Table Manners
(or the lack of Table Manners)

By Ray Tempus

Table Manners (or the lack of Table Manners)

Published By
One Temptation Press
545 Eighth Ave. Suite #401
New York, New York 10018
onetpress@yahoo.com

www.40points.com

ISBN: 978-0-9772587-4-1
First Printing: 2008

Acknowledgments

The Invisible Man Speaks. Thanks Folks. You know who you are. As always Sherry, Rodlyn, Margarita, Jenna, Punkin & Anthony. Your importance is unerasable. To the family from your loving son & father, baby brother & crazy uncle, my works are always dedicated to you. (But not blamed on you). Again love to all the X's (crazy women) and I guess I should thank a couple of you. Special thanks to my friends, Mr. Malfi, Laura, Christine & Barbra for steadying the ship. Mitch, Debra and the good people at Blue Q. Thanks to my friend Marisa and thanks to Claire. Thank you Gus & Marina, Tulio & Santiago. None of this would be possible (and we're having fun with it), be it not for Doug Ward and the crew at 1Tpress.

Now the "In the wheel" phase of this process is in a whole different dimension. Therefore it requires it's own set of acknowledgements. For me writing is not at all like creating visual art. Painting, sculpture,

drawing etc, are all internal exercises. Writing or in my case ranting, is an external exercise. Therefore I must allow the world from which the materials arise to enter my blissful reclusive realm. Or shall I say I must come out of my shell and take-in the world. So it's off to Starbucks. I wish I wasn't so like everybody about this but I confess, they got me. The bionic coffee is one thing. But it's the people that make it work. To start, they speak English. This is not anti-immigrant bull but at least you know the people are paid a legal wage with a few benefits and you know the company pays it's fair amount of employee tax. It's an added bonus that a brilliant guy like Craig is there to offer a great idea that contributes greatly to the remaining 17(or so) books in this series. Thanx man! Super Special warm fuzzy Thank yous to Pooja for reminding me to work. You'd make a great coach. (remind me I have 17 more books to go). Mary, Janette, Twin, Deslyn, Keisha, Isabel and Sparkle I'm so taken by your sweetness I don't know how to say thank you. That includes Devin and Lydia, good

luck with school. I saved a special space for Makeisha and Ama because your dazzling smiles and sparkling eyes melt my heart the way only my darling nieces can. Shawn and Enrique, gotta holla. Thanx Sarah and Eric for your encouragement and Ashley for not killing me for including you in the last book with out you knowing. And, as before thank you Hattie Hightower for getting the party started.

P.S. I haven't forgotten anyone, there are 17 more books to go in the series. I didn't want to forget to mention that.

Table of Contents

Introduction

Table Manners

... or shall we say the lack of.

By Ray Tempus

This book is an extension of a subject covered in my "launching pad" book, *Last One Gone Turn The Lights Out.*

I felt the need to be more complete after reviewers of the above mentioned expressed a desire to "read on", in a few of the chapters. They ask for more, so I shall.

I'll cover Table Manners first because I find it of the utmost importance.

Our society has no class. You can tell by the acute lack of table manners had by the greater majority of the population. 99% plus are clueless to "proper" table manners; o.k., but 98 percent seem to be downright pigs. This must be fixed.

We'll take you as close to correct as possible, hoping you fall somewhere between piggery and snobbery.

The fancy finishing school techniques are actually cool when you realize the social indications as well as class identification associated with this snobbery. While we will offer a reasonably good lesson in this snobbery, we won't quite elevate you to hob nobbery.

The idea here is to rid ourselves of beastly behavior like nose blowing and other awful things that happen at the table, be it home or out dining. But first I just gotta ask; you nose blowers, what the hell is wrong with you filthy beasts? You don't inherently know to never ever do that?

Now, just think of how many classless nasty asses you know. Give em' this damn book and make em' pay you for it.

Table Setting

don't panic

This will be simplified

Here we go again.....
from your crazy uncle who's
kept on the back porch.

Table Setting

The purpose here is not to teach the art of setting the table. However take notes as we all need to know the basics. Not only for entertaining. On the B.S. side you seem more sophisticated when dining out. On the real side you are more employable.

Don't be confused by the number of utensils; I know at home you use just one assisted by your fingers. Don't pick up forks asking, "what's this one for"? As courses come pick up utensils from the outside in. The top spoon is for after dinner coffee.

Simple rules on eating out

I don't wanna take too much time with this, I just need to point out one thing.

If you go some place to dine and someone seats you or o.k.'s your choice of seats and a person comes to your table to take your order, when you are done close your knife and fork. This tells the staff that you are finished. They will then come and clean the table. You leave a tip for the service. By the way, don't scrape or stack your dishes. Though you think you're showing good manners you're telling them that you're looking for a job busing tables.

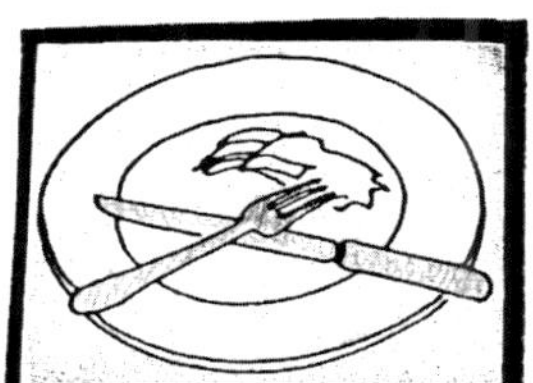

resting

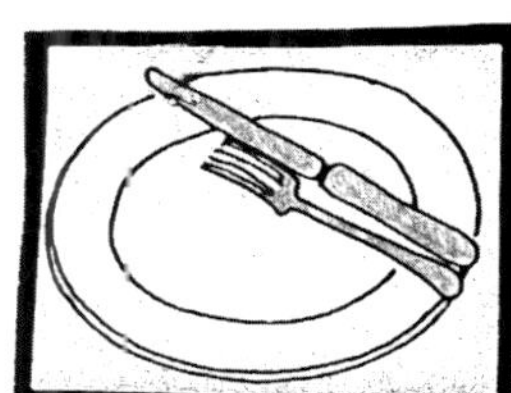

finished

If you go to a place where you go to a counter or whatever, order your food then take it to your table, (they usually have plastic utensils) when you're done throw your trash away. Why do you think they have big trash cans at the door as well as other locations throughout the place you idiot. And the people you see do this, delusional about who & what they are.

Left hand fork right hand knife you phony lowlife. AND DON'T LEAVE TIPS AT McDONALDS'S!!! JUST CLEAN YOUR TABLE!!

The Do's

(snobby mechanics)

Not to be snobbish, but poor table manners disgust me. First things first; left hand fork, right hand knife. This is not a lesson in technique, though it is of the utmost importance. Just let me say don't lace your fork between your fingers like a pencil, holding it food surface side up like a tiny shovel to skew and scoop the food maximum load. Let the knife assist the fork. No fingers.

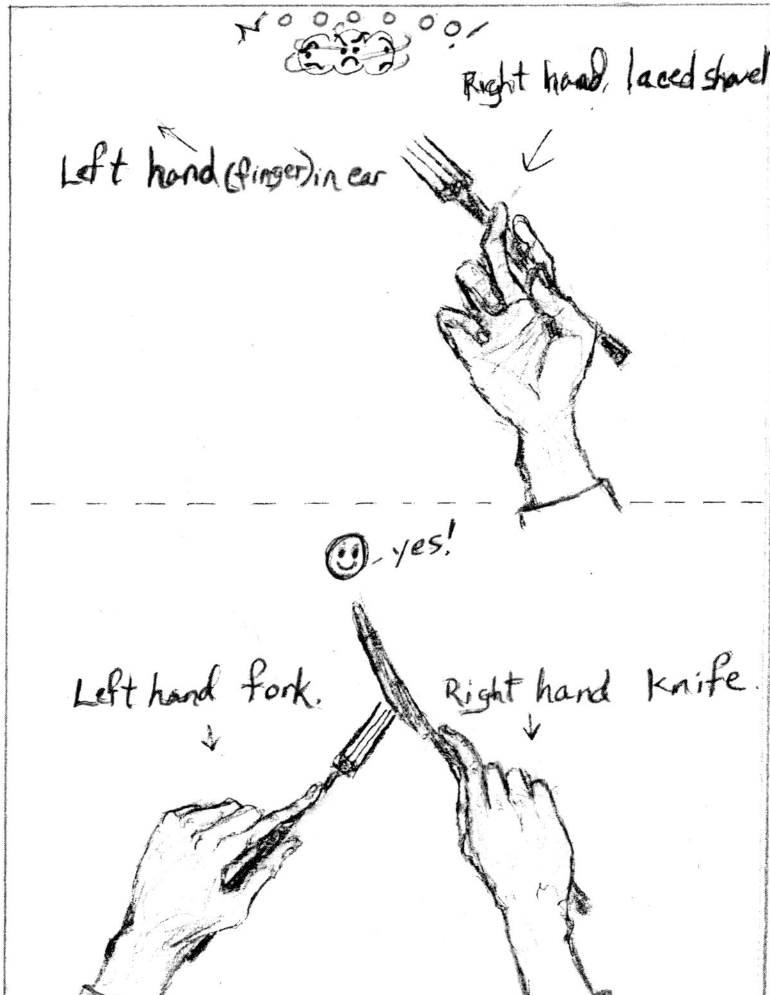
Right hand, laced shovel
Left hand (finger) in ear
yes!
Left hand fork.
Right hand knife.

Sit with good posture and bring the food to your mouth. Don't over load the fork rather skewing, scooping or both.

(top illustration)

Don't go down for the food or reach for it with your tongue.

(bottom illustration)

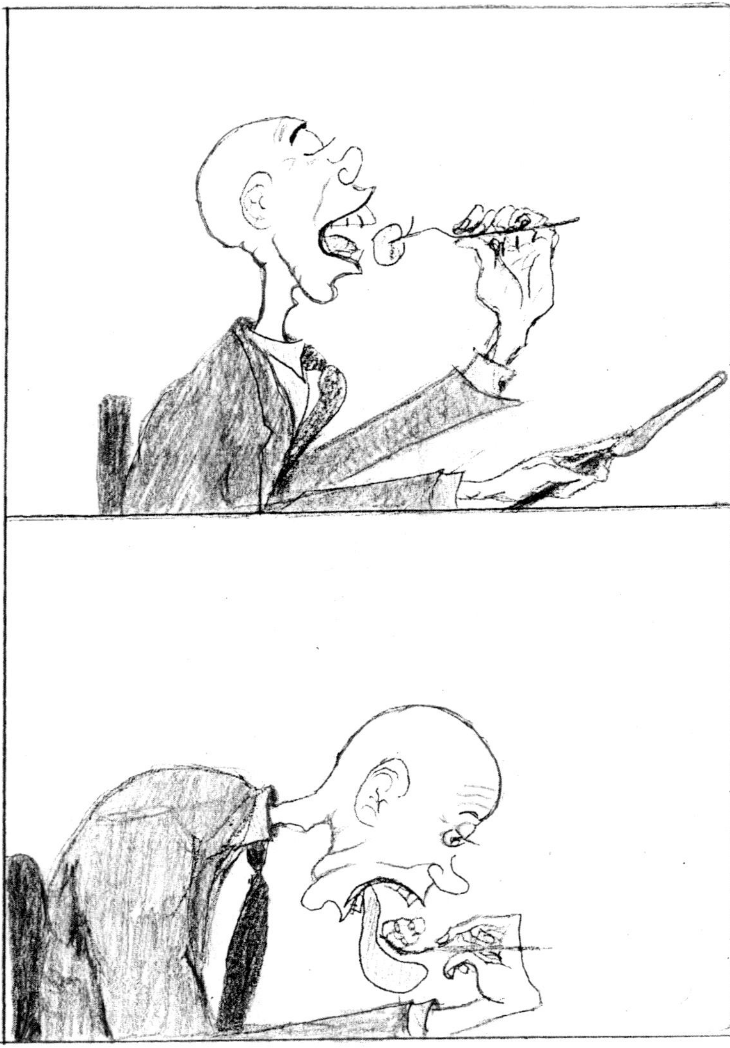

When having soup or other spoonables, spoon away from yourself.

(top illustration)

Always use your napkin correctly and you know about the elbows.

(bottom illustration)

Now, enough of the snobby mechanics. This is about more offensive behavior. Read on.

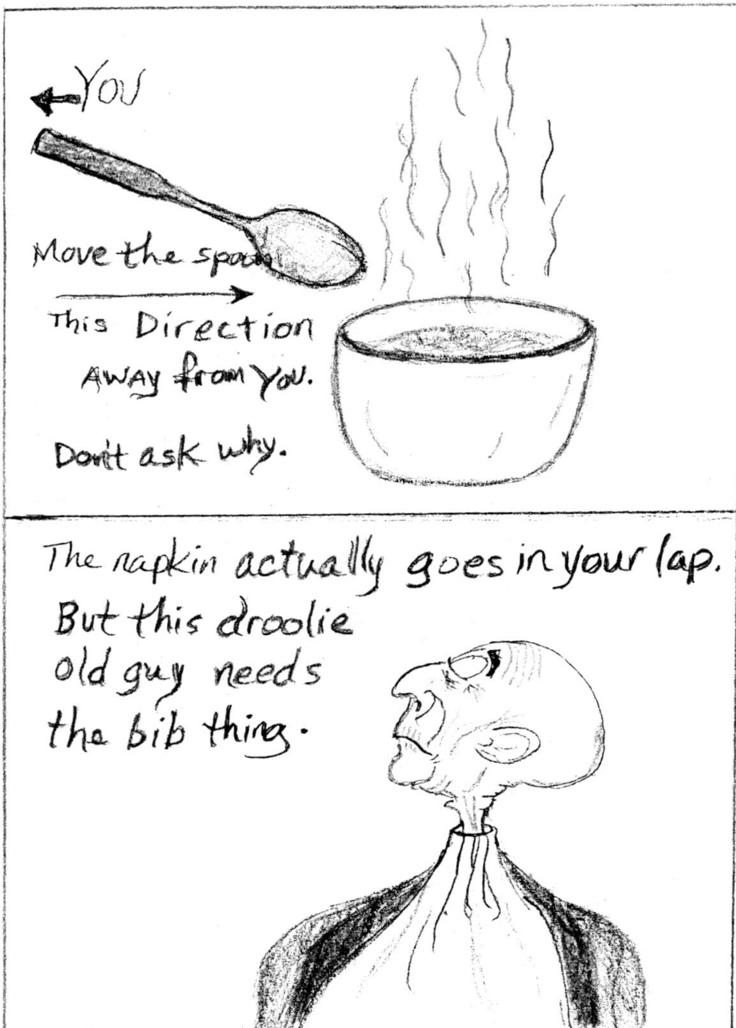
YOU
Move the spo
This Direction
AWAY from You.
Don't ask why.
The napkin actually goes in your lap.
But this droolie
old guy needs
the bib thing.

Now to the point
(Nose blowers and other disgusting slobs)

Check this out for yourself. Whenever you go to a restaurant to dine, be it a five star establishment or a seen-better-days grease bucket, at some point during your stay some nasty-ass is going to pull a snot-rag out of their nasty pocket and while at the table blow their nose loud and nastily. Yuck!! You think they care about the other people in the place? They don't even care about the people at their table.

Now this troll of a person may or may not be done at the time of the offence. Either way, one should excuse oneself to the restroom. Going outside would be o.k. but there's no sink. In the restroom you can wash your snotty hands. You certainly can't wash em' at the table.

This disgusting act should be punishable by a long period of wearing a 'I'm a booger swallower' T-shirt.

I AM A
BOOGER
SWALLOWER

Another thing, talking while leaning toward the table is kinda yukkie. Many people spit when they talk. UGH! Those specks of flying food. Puke! (see pg#29 & 31)

Lean back in your chair when you talk. Swallow your food first, then don't talk too loud. Use mild hand gestures for effect. Mild. Never clear your throat at the table.

If it's a classy joint and you hope to make a good impression on your dinner companions don't order anything that you pick up with your hands. (except bread). Reasons are many. And women shouldn't order meat. Especially the meat that when you're done the poor critters bones are left on your plate. Maybe it's just me, but it looks like such damage was done and there you sit looking fulfilled. Scary.

Things to never do when at the table.

There will be No....

- Ear picking.
  (Ear wax tastes awful. Don't act like you didn't know that.)
  (top illustration)

- Nose picking or touching.
  (ya' nasty ass nose blower)
  (bottom illustration)

- No scratching.

This is a big one. Scratching removes dead skin, releasing a fine invisible dust. Head scratching is worse. Out flies the dandruff and that's not always invisible. If someone does this slap em' and slap em' hard. Get up and leave. Stick em' with the check.

FOOD

- No coughing.

- No hocking.
  (same reason)

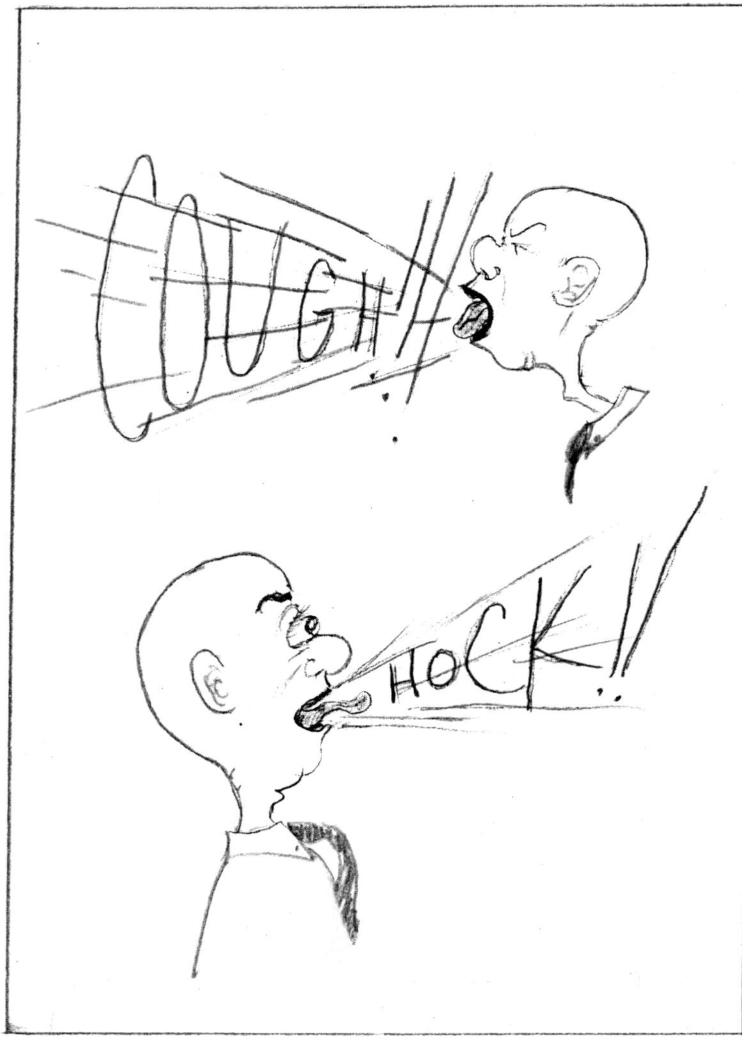
COUGH!!
HOCK!!

- No throat clearing. (top)
  (thoughtlessly nasty)

- Or Snorting. (bottom)
  (even nastier)

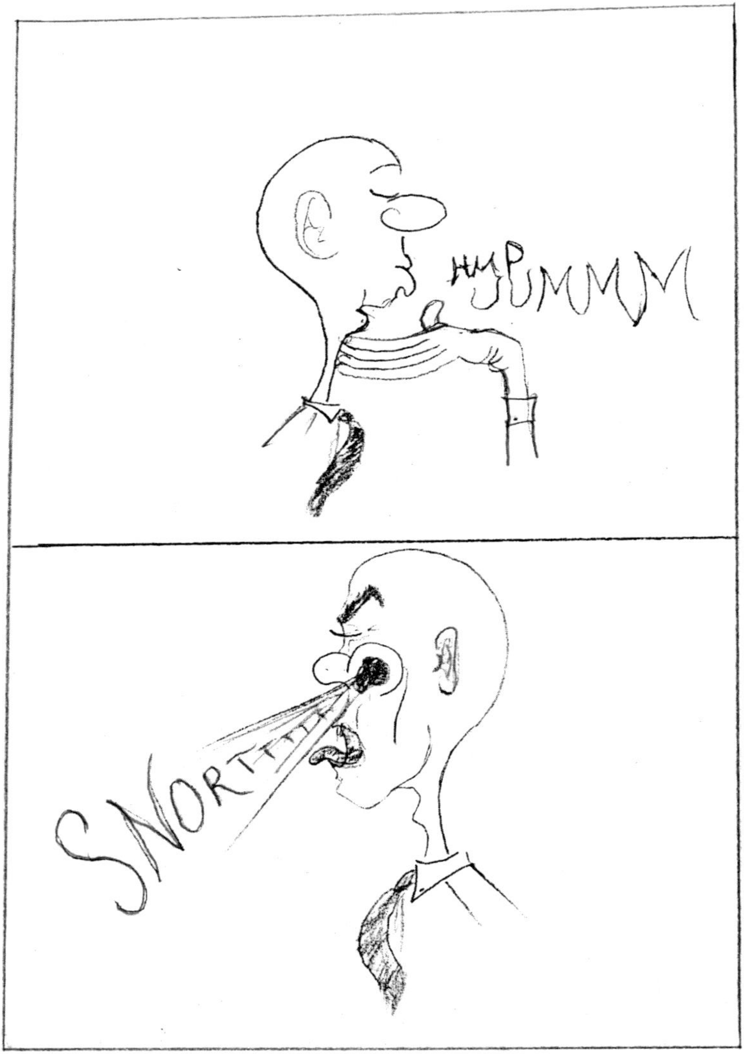
HMPUMMM
SNORTTTT

- No loud laughing (top)

or loud talking. (bottom)

Remember those specs of flying food? This is how they happen.

HAHAHAHA!
I, I, I, I,
Lie, Lie, Lie, Lie.
Yakity, Yakity

- No leaning on the table while talking.

(top illustration)

- No food in mouth talking.

(bottom illustration)

I'm sooo Cool.
•Note to the reader: If I even try to give you a visual image of this disgusting act, the act itself turns my stomach.
You've been spared.

- No Nasty talking.

This subject will be covered in greater detail in the soon to be released book, 'Get a room'. The subject was also covered in the "Launching Pad" book, [Last One Gone Turn The Lights Out] under the chapter heading, ['Overly Affectionate Couples In Public']
Remember, the reason these look-at-us couples behave this way in public is often times because neither of the ugly loser's has their own place.

Hey baby, ya
wanna
He He

- No kissing. (see fore mentioned)

(top illustration)

- No volume burping.

(bottom illustration)

GO HOME! or GET A ROOM!
You wet kissn' booty grabbinguglies.
BURP!

- No Stinking. (figure it out)

  (top illustration)

- No tooth picking.

  (bottom illustration)

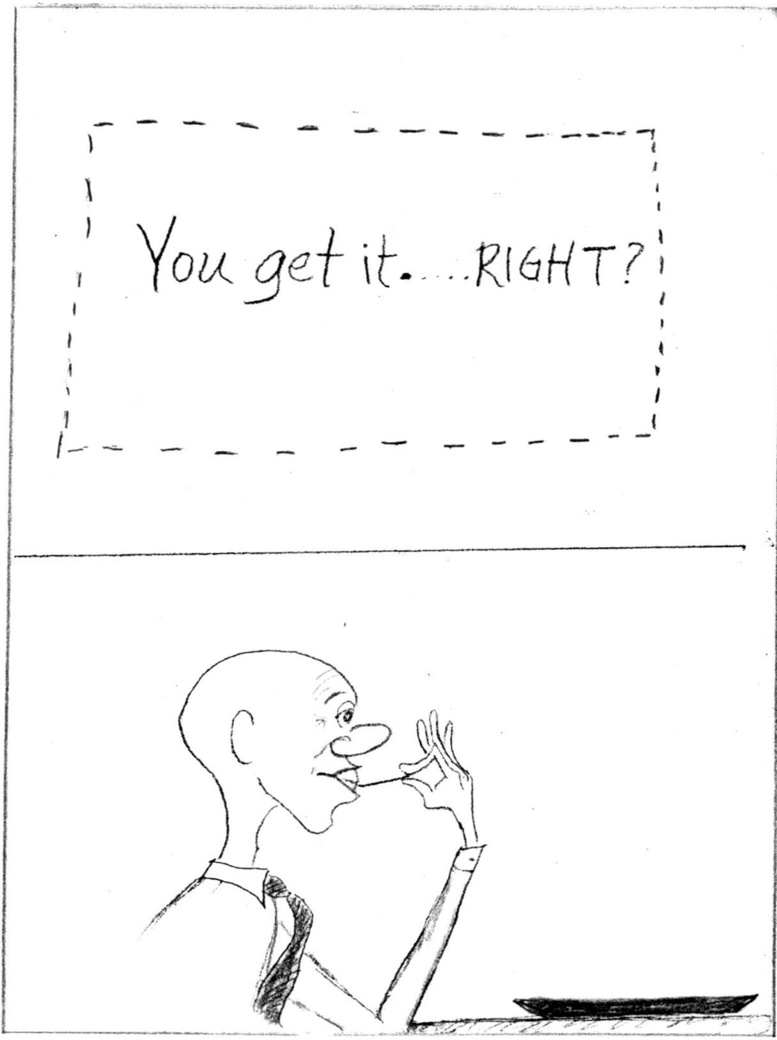
You get it.....RIGHT?

- No Farting (Duh)
  (top)

- or easing out quiet farts.
  (they stink worse and you know it)
  (bottom)

LET'S KEEP it CLEAN.
NO VISUAL NESSASARRY
...We're staying the course here.

- No hair management.

No matter how cute you are...
... well ... o.k.
Some of you LADIES can get away with this one.

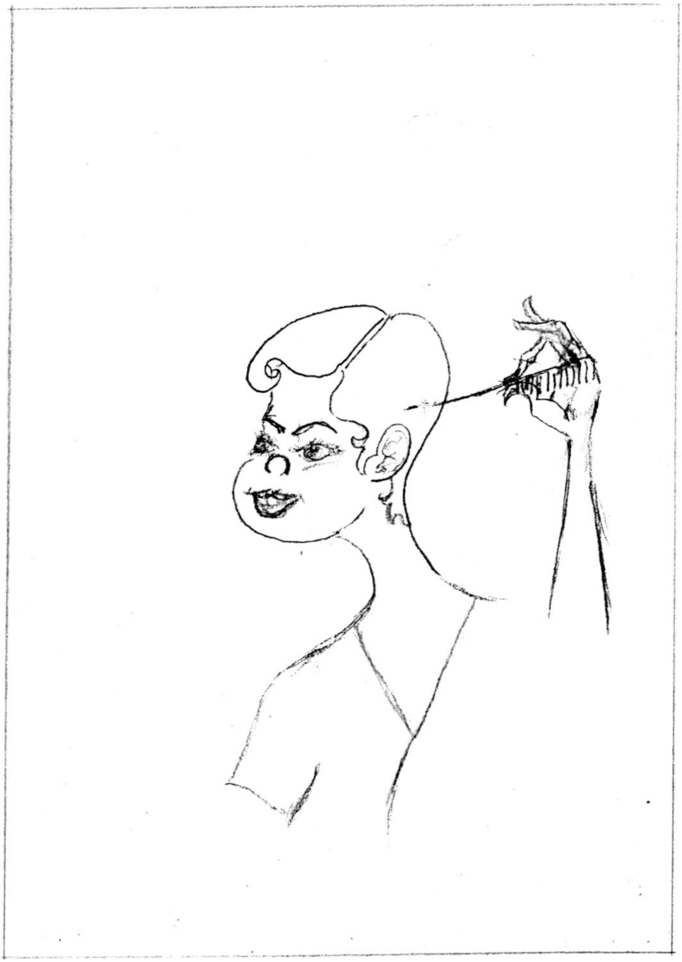

- No fingernail clicking.
  (ladies I hope)

- No facial hair touching.
  (fellas I hope)

- No Sneezing.
  (top illustration)

- No Sneeze stopping. (runaway)
  (middle & bottom illustration)

AHHHHH!
ChOOOOOOO!
Sneezing
Sneeze stopping
No!
Run away from the table?
YES!

- No Drooling.
(slobberers look real dumb)

- No yawning.
(can you say breath mints?)

- No Elbows on the table.
  (oldest rule in the book)

Well, kinda. I don't think it's the first rule, but it's the one you heard the most. Most people don't know why elbows shouldn't be on the table, but still know about this because they've heard it a zillion times. Don't ask why just keep em' off.

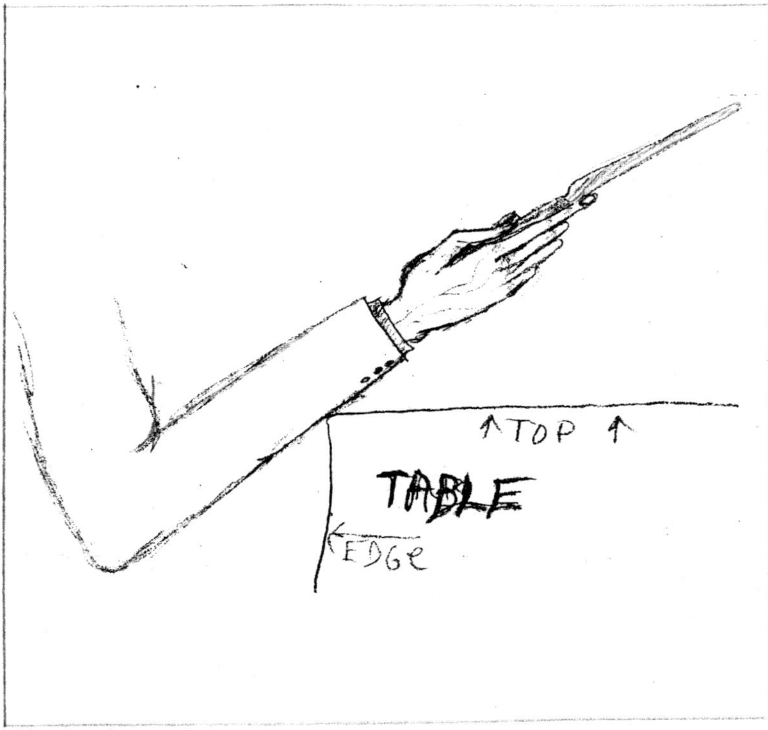
TOP
TABLE
EDGE

Awful things you can kinda get away with.

- Easing out a silent burp is sort of o.k. as long as it doesn't smell.

- Dozing off is o.k. if you're leaning back in your chair and are balanced.

While it tells your boring company that they are in fact boring, you can do no more harm while sleeping. Unless you slobber, or a fart jumps out.

FAAART

This_ _ _ _actually happened.

Here's an example of when dozing off is not o.k.

One evening when out dining with a group of six people, (three men three women), kind of an informal meeting of artist and art dealers. In such groups dozing off is really no big deal and one little fellow in the group dozed off three or four minutes after our food arrived. Though he was leaning back in his chair and balanced, he was much too close to the table for what happened to him.... or should I say happened to us.

Poor little fellow went into a violent coughing attack. Not just his food was contaminated, the whole damn table was blanked up. We were all repulsed and disgusted. Of course the attack woke his lil' ass up. He realized what he'd done and was so ashamed. He apologized profusely. While everyone seemed to really feel sorry for the lil guy there was no way to hide the disgust. Needless to say dinner was over.

I can't help but recall one puzzling dining experience. Two companions and myself found ourselves in a summer resort-town café in the winter. Luckily we were the only patrons. Because I would've hated to have been "one of those ill mannered city people", who even come to ruin lunch in winter.

The other male in our party received a call on his cell. We'd already placed our order so to be polite he went outside to talk. Our food arrived so we had the table attendant cover his food. My friend and I proceeded to dine. Her gracious table manners were no surprise as she is a cultured and tasteful woman. Luckily we'd finished our food before our companion returned. After being outside for nearly an hour he came in, sat down, uncovered his plate, took the napkin and blew like a foghorn. Then properly placed the napkin in his lap. Why didn't he blow his nose outside?.... To be drawn & quartered.

The worse incident was the time I was on a date with what I thought was a wonderful lady. Fooled me. The perfect lady from the

I'M OUTTA HERE!
YUCK!
BLAH BLAH BLAH, YAKKITY YAKKITY YAKKITY - I'M SO WONDERFUL

time we met until three minutes into this meal. I'm overlooking the tacky handling of utensils. She did the eye booger thing. ... and pulled the string. Well blow ya' nose why don't cha!

Had to get outta there. I reached under the table and under my pant leg to snatch a couple of hairs from my leg. I put the hairs on my plate, pointed them out to her, called for the waitress and complained quietly. I refused to allow a new dish to be brought and I refused to pay for my dinner. I paid for hers technically but saw it as paying only for my own and not eating it.

Now the Miss America that did the loud gurgly blow in the middle of dining was worse. But that nasty girl has been erased from my memory. After all that I won't even mention the classy gentleman who looked the casual yet rich young for a grandpa type. Classy that is, until he took his index finger and used it as a utensil. Mr. CEO was digging into a large cup and scooping out the contents, then licking and sucking his fingers until the next enthusiastic dig. The guy went at it like a crazed maniac til

the very last drop. Then licked his hand for several minutes.

But after those nose blowers this crazy guy doesn't even warrant our attention.

Now ya' got it.

(How to handle nasty violators of decency)

What to do if:

- You get an eye booger puller...see pg.54.
- You get a whooping' cougher...see pg.52.
- You get a sneezer... stop eating and hate em' for life.
- You get a nose blower... tell em' of your disgust, leave the table and tell their mother.
- You get a scratcher...stick em' with the check.
- You get a farter...shoot em' dead.
- You get a spit talker... don't eat that!
- You get an elbower... spread nasty rumors about em'.
- You get kissers... smack em'.
- You get a nose or ear picker... call the cops.
- You get a throat clearer... hire a bunch of hooligans to beat the hell out of em'.
- You get a loud burper... stick them with the check too.

- You get a slobberer… smash em' in the face with a pie.
- You get a tooth picker… same thing, pie in the eye.
- Someone at your table drops dead… move to another table.

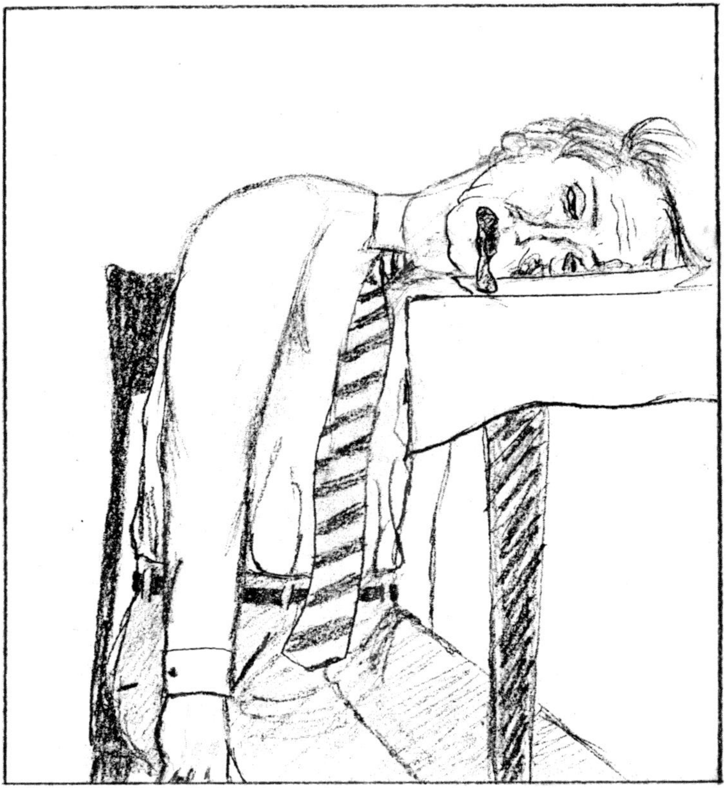

All bets are off!!!

When....

FART!!

All bets are off....

When you want out of the marriage "all bets are off. Anything goes. Except elbows on the table. Burpin, fart'n, cuss'n, stink'n, whatever. Blow your nose on the table cloth...(at home). Just watch the elbows.

- When you're alone; same thing. But, &<!@ the elbows. Yo name is Fred. Just don't make yourself sick. (pg. 60 illustration)

- When you're at a place with plastic utensils you don't need to do the finishing school thing but the other niceties are expected. Unless the place has an ugly old lady that makes the place a real dive. Case in point: You recall the place I describe as Cheers in "Last One Gone Turn The Lights Out".

You know, neighborhood pub feel when the regulars are around. Well the restaurant part is good, the bar could be too. ... But.

I'd mentioned the beautiful young woman in charge who handled fighting patrons without incident.

Well, she ain't there anymore. Now the bartender is Wrinklestiltskin. A really ugly old monster who encourages as well as picks fights with patrons. What a dive!

This from a wrinkled old leprechaun looking woman with a heavy Irish brogue. Ugly as sin and mean as hell. Table manners? "All bets are off"! You can even forget the elbows.

- By the third helping "all bets are off". Hell you might as well take your shoes off by now.

Speaking of Family....

Holidays, Weddings, BBQ's,
Sundays, whatever.....

ALL BETS ARE OFF!

With the exception of nose blowing and the extreme nasties, anything goes.

From sitting on the floor barefooted eating with your fingers to stealing food off your brothers plate it's all good baby. There's no place like home.

HOME
SWEET
HOME

OH YEAH......
(I almost forgot)

There will be no:

- As spoken, No eye booger picking!
  (top illustration)

- No underarm sniffing.
  (bottom illustration)

See page #54
We needn't sicken you twice

- No underarm exposing.

(top illustration)

- No bone sucking. Veg it!

(bottom illustration)

- No arguing. Leave the politics for street corners;... so you can fight.

(top illustration)

- No sick stomach looks. No matter how bad the food is.

(bottom illustration)

Politics?
CHEQUE
$
DOG FOOD?

- No speed eating.

(top)

- No holding food in midair on a utensil while talking or listening. When you put food on a utensil eat it.

(bottom)

BLAH BLAH
BLAH BLAH BLAH
BLAH BLAH
BLAH
BLAH—
GRUB

In Parting

So remember, table manners are nothing more than treating others kindly. Don't give anybody the icky's. Wait until everyone's food has been served before you eat.

All the stuff about serving to the left or right or whatever isn't for me to go into. I'm just trying to keep you from blowing your nose at the table. The silverware handling is to make it seem like you had good upbringing.

And do remember to always dab your mouth good with your napkin before taking a sip of water, wine or whatever. Otherwise you'll leave sickening chewed food goop on the rim of the glass. Yuck! Use the napkin. I understand that it's o.k. to share food even at a restaurant. Well you're not getting any of mine.

Now you are not only ready to dine out, you are also ready to identify classless lowlife's no matter their socio-economic or whatever else class. Money, level of education, style of

dress, race, creed, or color have nothing to do with it.

America is full of rich Scumbags. No, wealth doesn't make you a lowlife nor does the lack of it. No one knows this better than the cultured well-to-do. Money is just money. (nicer to have it). Being, "broke" is an economic condition that can change with will and determination, or luck. Poor is a state of mind and behavior.

If you're rich so what, if you are not so what. Have a little class. The End.

P.S. If you hear anyone say, "lemme get" or 'can I get", you have a lowlife of poor upbringing. Spare me the details. Now....

The End

P.S...

Ray's Middle Finger

Welcome to the first installment of:

Ray's middle finger.

Ray's middle finger is somewhere between the SNL skit, "Mr. Robinson's Neighborhood" (Eddie Murphy) and Al Goldstein's "*?@$ you". (Midnight Blue).

You were all fairly warned on the very last page of *Last One Gone Turn The Lights Out*. I told you don't make my next book! You can only earn this by being a deplorable lowlife.

Meet Shawn the scumbag. (This is not the same Shawn as the cool guy in acknowledgments). Since the punk-ass is a nobody I'll tell you where to reach him and tell him he's vomit. Everybody at Starbucks ain't o.k., and I've given the company enough props. Ya' got bad apples too. The vermin Shawn, exploits a poor homeless old drug addled bag-lady for sex. Either that or the bum is dealing dope to her. What other reasons could there be for the two of them sneaking into the bathroom together after the bathroom's are closed for cleaning? Prayer?

I don't think he's dealing dope. I'll bet a hundred dollars to a dime it's sex. He's the night Manager, she's the homeless old lady who sits by the window sleeping. On his cue she goes to a closed section toward the restrooms. He then disappears to the back for the rendezvous. There are really no barricades, so you can see where they go. Ten to fifteen minutes later they emerge. Him grinning behind the counter, her (now with coffee money) back to the window seat, but now she has cake and coffee. Hhhmmm?

Well it don't take a bright white boy to figure this one out. Shawn-boy is vermin! Shawn is a really fat tall guy with coa-coa brown skin and a very short neat haircut. (I'll betcha his mother is as fat and ugly as he is). The bag lady, (foul old skunk) is a puny drug addict with splotchy greasy looking pinky skin. Her hair is a mix of grey and dirty blonde. She has an acidic odor of urine. This stinking duo can be avoided by not going to the w67th st. at Columbus Ave. Starbucks in NYC at night. This is double the reason this loser Shawn gets

Ray's middle finger. The location is in the heart of NY's most popular entertainment venue, Lincoln Center for the Performing Arts. After enjoying the best cultural events available it's nice to have a relaxing cup-a-joe with friends before heading home. I'll not go there again! Been three times, two times this happened. The other time Shawn wasn't there. I don't blame the bag lady, she's a victim of herself and Shawn.

So here's to Shawn; die you fat stinking lowlife. Die with oozing bumps you rat-fink. Should you happen to speak to this zero (212) 721-0470 tell him Ray said F-you punk.

Now ya know. Annoy the crazy guy and you too will get... Ray's Middle Finger.

Thanks Honey
You still owe me a quarter punk!

Books by Ray Tempus:

- A 40 Point Guide To Peeing In New York
- Last One Gone Turn The Lights Out
- Table Manners (or the lack of Table Manners)

Coming Titles in a 20 Book Series:

- Phony As A 3$ Bill
- Lemme Get
- Gone To The Dogs
- Get A Room
- The Daily Commute
- Weed N' Whisky (Reefer, reefer madness & mad cow)
- If You See Em' Call The Cops
- The Devil Totes A Bible
- Economics 101
- Just For The Record
- On ISMS (The Government's trying to kill us all)
- The Corporate Takeover

- Celebrate This ?@!* (Tempus On Celebrity Culture)
- Go Home (Tempus on Immigration and Migration)
- The Hob Knobs (High Society)
- Where Are The Cops ? (Scammers, Schemers, Snake Oil Sellers, Pyramiders, Dirty Dealers, Hooks, Crooks & Dastardly Lying Lowlifes, wear business suits.) *with flagpens.*
- Edumacation (Who Stole The Curriculum)

Next Ray Tempus Book:

... Well, on this page in Last One Gone Turn The Lights Out I said the next book would be, "Phony As A 3$ Dollar bill". So I guess I should declare the next book to be, "Phony As A 3$ Dollar Bill".

But don't be surprised to get,

"Weed N' Whisky"